Options Trading Crash Course And Strategies

The Complete Beginner's Guide With Most Effective
Illustrated Strategies For Investing With Options And
Generating Passive Income

Byron McGrady

Table of Contents

Introduction 8

CHAPTER 1: Options Contract 10

CHAPTER 2: Securities 16

    Cash and Bank Security 17

    Certificate of Deposit 17

    Stocks 18

    Bonds 19

    Real Estate... 19

    Precious Metals... 20

    Derivatives 20

    Investing Strategies... 21

        Buy and Hold 21

        Value Investment 22

        Growth Investing... 23

CHAPTER 3: Debit And Credit Spreads 24

    Debit Spread 24

        Types of Debit Spreads 25

    Credit Spread 26

        Types of Credit Spreads 27

CHAPTER 4: Options Strategies: Going Long vs. Going Short................28

    Long Position.. 28

Simple Going Long Strategies 30

    Long Call..30

    Long Put 32

Short Position 34

    Short Call...36

CHAPTER 5: The Flexibility Of Options **38**

Understanding Flexible Exchange Option (FLEX)........................38

Parts of a FLEX Option Contract 40

Position Limits for Flexible Exchange Options...........................40

CHAPTER 6: Strangles Strategies **42**

What Are the Advantages of This Strategy?...............................45

CHAPTER 7: Straddle Strategies **48**

CHAPTER 8: Covered Call **54**

Benefits of Covered Call Options..55

Risks of Covered Call Options 55

Covered Calls Involve A Long Position 56

Covered Calls Are A Neutral Strategy 57

How to Create a Covered Call Option...57

An Example Of A Covered Call 58

CHAPTER 9: Strategies for Selling Covered Call **62**

Bear Put Spread Strategy..62

    Execution 63

Bull Put Spread Strategy...65

    Execution 65

Put Calendar Spread Strategy...67

    Choices..68

    Purpose...69

CHAPTER 10: Iron Condor **70**

Execution.. 72

Example... 75

Easy Formula 77

CHAPTER 11: Options Pricing **78**

Strike Price and Underlying Price............................... 79

Factors That Affect An Option's Price 81

History Of The Black-Scholes Model 82

Stock Price... 83

Strike Price 83

Type Of Option.. 84

Time To expiration 85

Interest Rates 85

Dividends... 87

Volatility 87

CHAPTER 12: Dividends **88**

What Are Dividends? 88

Dividend Investing... 89

Comparing Stocks for Dividend Investing 90

When to Reinvest or Not to Reinvest 90

Dividend Growth Investing: Case Study....................... 91

How to Start Chasing Dividend Income 92

Pick a Type of Account 92

Choose a Stockbroker 92

Decide between ETFs and Stocks............................. 93

Keep on Contributing and Investing 93

CHAPTER 13: Technical Analysis For Options Trading **94**

Studying Trends with Moving Averages 94

Momentum..98

Support and Resistance 100

Breakouts..102

Trendlines 103

Conclusion **105**

Introduction

The world of finance can be a complicated place, but it doesn't have to be. Options Trading is a great way to get involved in the world of finance without the heavy learning curve.

This guide will introduce you to Options Trading basics, and how it fits into the world of financial markets. We'll show you what options are, how they work, and how you can use them to your advantage.

It is one of the most profitable and exciting ways to earn money. Although options trading can be complicated, it is not difficult to understand. In this article, we'll cover the basics, strategies, and information you need to know about options trading.

Options trading is similar to investing in stocks and bonds, except instead of buying shares of a company or buying paper for cash; you are buying an option on it.

Options trading is a type of derivative trade. It is the practice of buying and selling options contracts to control the price of stocks, commodities, indices, foreign currency, and other financial assets. Options are financial securities that give the holder the right to buy or sell a particular asset at a specific price and date.

It can be used to gain exposure to particular asset classes without having to purchase the underlying investments. They also provide traders with an opportunity to control their risk when trading a high-risk investment asset.

Options trading is an innovative way to invest in the market. Traders can profit from both rising and falling prices of stocks.

Options trading continues to gain popularity. It is becoming easier for first-time investors to enter this lucrative market through online brokerages, and discount brokerages like Options Trading Crash Course Online Brokerage (Options Trading Crash Course).

CHAPTER 1:

Options Contract

We will now introduce the concept of options contracts, and how they are used in the stock market. The most basic way to get involved in option involves buying options contracts based on bets you make on whether future stock prices will rise or fall.

An options contract is a pretty simple concept.

- It's a contract. That means it's a legal agreement between a buyer and a seller.

- It allows the purchaser of the contract to purchase or dispose of an asset with a fixed amount.

- The purchase is optional, so the buyer of the contract does not have to buy or sell the asset.

- The contract has an expiration date, so the purchaser must make the trade before the expiration date once they choose to exercise their right.

The purchaser of the contract pays a non-refundable fee for the contract. Some options contracts take place in all aspects of daily life, including real estate and speculation. A simple example illustrates the concept of an options contract.

Suppose you are itching to buy a BMW, and you've decided the model you want must be silver. You drop by a local dealer, and it turns out they don't have a stock. The dealer affirms he can get you by the end of the month. You say you'll take the car if the dealer can get it by the last day of the month, and sell it to you for $67,500. He agrees and requires you to put a $3,000 deposit on the car.

If the last day of the month arrives and the dealer hasn't produced the car, you're freed from the contract and get your money back. In the event he does deliver the vehicle at any date before the end of the month, you have the option to buy it or not. If you wanted the car, you could buy it, but of course, you can't be forced to buy the car, and maybe you've changed your mind in the interim.

The right is there but not the obligation to purchase. In short, no pressure if you decided not to push through with the car's purchase. However, if you choose to let the opportunity pass since the dealer met his end of the bargain and produced the car, you lose the $3,000 deposit.

In this case, the dealer, who plays the contract writer's role, must follow through with the sale based upon the agreed-upon price.

Suppose that when the car arrives at the dealership, BMW announces it will no longer make silver cars. As a result, the prices of new silver BMWs that were the last ones to roll off the assembly line skyrocket. Other dealers are selling their BMWs for $100,000. However, since this dealer entered into an options contract with you, he must sell the car to you for the pre-agreed price of $67,500. You decide to get the car and drive away, smiling, knowing that you saved $32,500 and sell it at a profit if you wanted to. The situation here captures the essence of options contracts, even if you've never thought of negotiating with a car dealer in those terms.

An option is a kind of bet. In the car's example, the dealer can deliver the particular vehicle you want within the stated period and at the agreed-upon price. The dealer is betting too. He bets that the pre-agreed cost is a good one for him. Of course, if BMW stops making silver cars, then he's made the wrong bet.

It can work the other way too. Let's say that instead of BMW deciding not to make silver cars anymore when your vehicle is being driven onto the lot, another car crashes into it. Now your silver BMW has a small dent on the rear bumper with some scratches. As a result, the vehicle has immediately declined in value. But if you want the car, since you've agreed to the options contract, you must pay $67,500, even though with the dent, it's only really worth $55,000. You can walk away and lose your $3,000 or pay what is now a premium price on a damaged car.

Another example that is commonly used to explain options contracts is purchasing a home built by a developer under the agreement that certain conditions are met. The buyer will be required to put a non-refundable down payment or deposit on the home. Let's say that the developer agrees to build them the house for $300,000, provided that a new school is made within 5 miles of the development within one year. So, the contract expires within a year. During the year, the buyer can go forward with the construction of the home for $300,000 if the school is built.

The developer has agreed to the price no matter what. So if the housing market in general and construction of the school, in particular, drive up demand for housing in the area, and the developer is selling new homes that are now priced at $500,000, he has to sell this home for $300,000 because that was the price agreed to when the contract was signed.

The home buyer got what they wanted, being within 5 miles of the new school, with the home price fixed at $300,000. The developer was assured of the sale but missed out on the unknown, which was the skyrocketing price due to increased demand. If the school isn't built, and the buyers don't exercise their option to buy the house before the contract expires at one year, the developer can pocket the $20,000 cash.

In the car case, the buyer is hoping to get the vehicle they want at what they perceive to be a bargain price, although if BMW stopped making silver cars, they might sell it to a third party and then get a white one from the dealer. However, in most cases, the buyer wants the car. That isn't the case when it comes to options with stocks.

On the stock market, we are betting on the future price itself, and the shares of stock will be bought or sold at a profit if things work out. The critical point is the buyer of the options contract is not hoping to acquire the shares and hold them for an extended period like a traditional investor. Instead, you're hoping to make a bet on the stock price, secure that price, and then be able to trade the shares on that price no matter what happens in the actual markets.

CHAPTER 2:

Securities

Everyone who wants to avoid being broke or living from payslip to payslip must have the right investment strategy. An investment strategy is a plan for making the money you already have to multiply to more money.

Suitable investments have to have liquidity, meaning that whatever you invest in has to be easily convertible into cash at hand. Investments are risky, though, meaning that it's not guaranteed to always get your intended profits because, at any time, your assets can devalue. Therefore, it is essential to carefully examine your investments and see how much it's likely to yield; this is called looking at the potential returns. Looking through all these possibilities will help a person determine what type of investment to go for.

An investment strategy is best if it works to meet your needs. Do not go for investment only because it's trending; it may not work for you. Going for what works for you will ensure that you stick to your investment for long, and swayed away by other trends. The best way to find an investment that works for you is by getting something that defines you, and that would be something you patient about.

It is good for young people to take more risks in investments by going for high growing stock investments. While someone who is about to retire, they must take fewer risks and distribute their assets to bonds.

A security type is the kind of investment you hold, and it should always be diverse.

Cash and Bank Security

This type has very high liquidity because you are dealing with cash at hand that you take to the bank and withdraw at will. It has a low risk because unless you need the money, it is safely kept at the bank. However, this means that it has no potential for growth, and can even lose its value if there is inflation. The most significant advantage with this, however, is that you have access at any needed time. Banks also offer emergency funds, and therefore in case you urgently need money, you do not have to wait for long.

Certificate of Deposit

The liquidity in this is low because you cannot withdraw cash whenever you want. You can only get the money after the agreed time with the bank. The risk is low because the money is safely kept at the bank. However, its growth potential is very minimal since it has a specified rate of interest. This means that your money is lying in a bank waiting for a specific interest rate instead of taking chances elsewhere. The growth rate is so low and not worth the time you waited to get the interest.

Stocks

Whenever people think about investments, they think of stocks. The liquidity is high because you get to buy shares from a company and share their profits. You can purchase shares from one or as many companies as possible, and therefore get to enjoy a certain percentage of their earnings. The risk is medium because you are also involved with their losses as much as you want the profits. Thus, this means that you should not expect to be paid when the company you have shared with is not making profits. However, all investments go through this uncertainty; no single investment won't have a loss risk. The potential for growth in this is very high as you grow, the more the company grows. Every company's objective is to yield profits, and therefore companies will continue putting their best foot forward to make sure they do not incur losses. The more they work on this, the more their profits. The more the company's profits, the more your shares, therefore, why the potential growth is high.

Bonds

The liquidity in this is medium because it involves getting to give some of your money as a loan to a company or government. Then after the agreed time, your money is returned to you along with the interest you agreed on. The interest rates may be very high or low, depending on whom you have loaned. If you lend big companies or treasury, you are much secured, and therefore the returns in this are small. The risk comes in because you may give loans to what is known as junk bonds, and you risk not being paid or having partial payments. However, since junk bonds do not guarantee security, they make sure to offer a little higher return than a large corporate that ensures security. The growth potential is medium because it depends on the profits you make from the payments.

Real Estate

The liquidity is low because it involves lands and buildings. Converting lands and buildings is dependent on the value the assets have accumulated over time. If you need to have cash from these investments, you have to make sure you are selling at a better price than you used when buying them. This makes the risk medium because they are assets, and may either maintain their value or grow. If they fail, it is a disadvantage to the investor, but if the assets increase in value, then the investor has made it. Growth potential is medium because of how long it takes to generate value finally.

Precious Metals

The liquidity is very high because it involves buying precious metals like gold and silver. When you buy precious metals, you can easily convert them into cash by selling them at an even higher price than you bought them. The risk is medium because the metals need a lot of proper handling to ensure that they do spoil, and also most buyers tend to buy at very low prices. The potential growth is medium because it depends on the available market and the demand as well.

Derivatives

The liquidity is medium. You can either convert your earnings quickly, depending on how accessible the stocks you bought are. Here you get to purchase stocks from another stock instead of making a direct purchase. And for this to happen, you have to believe that the stock you are buying will increase its value. The risk is very high because you depend on another stock to earn your profits without being directly involved. If the stock does not allow you to buy in a more valuable stock, then you are unlikely to make any value out of it. However, the growth potential is very high since you only get to buy from stocks with value.

It is important to be diverse in your investments; this means you do not settle on a particular type. If you can split your assets, you are in a better secure position. When there is a downfall in one sector, you can count on another industry. But if you hold all your assets in one industry and the sector goes down, you will significantly suffer as an investor because you will lose everything. Something else worth noting is that one should be careful with their investment as they get older. One mistake from such a person can lead them into a very desperate life after retirement.

Investing Strategies

Buy and Hold

This calls for thorough research before entirely going into any investment. After the research, you should settle for a long-term investment of like ten years. You should then buy this investment, and hold it irrespective of how many temptations that you may come through along the way to sell them. Sometimes it may be so tempting to sell it because the price you are being offered is a little tempting, but you should be able to resist. An investor should only sell if the rules for sticking to the stock are no longer favorable.

This may happen in that either there is a sign that the stocks are no longer maintainable. This could be because the company is taking a different strategy than what you signed up for, and there you get uncomfortable to continue. You may also sell only. If you have had enough before the end of the long-term and you want to opt-out. It should never be out of greed, thinking that what you are being offered is too good to resist because you do not know how much better you will get.

You may do significant research and have everything correctly figured out. You may yield your investments after the long-term you had invested in. However, when retirement sinks in, you need the money urgently because that's your only survival hope. The other downside is that you may have made the wrong choice all along. With a buy and hold strategy, you may make a lot of loss that will kick you out of the market even if unwilling to.

Value Investment

This means that you go for stocks that are more underestimated than the other stocks. In short, it means going for stocks that most people are unlikely to go for. This is risky but brave because you are not following the crowd. In doing this, you go for companies that are just beginning to grow, and have not attracted the big fish in the market; you can also go for only recently established companies. You can stick to this investment until you feel that you are doing quite well or have achieved more than you expected before eventually selling. This, however, does not come without a possible risk, as explained below.

Being an active trader makes you have easy, quick access to more significant returns. However, that also means that it's also very easy and fast to make losses as quick as it is to make profits. Therefore, it is usually recommended that you use small investments instead of putting in too much for this kind of trading because anything can happen. It is better to lose little than to lose hugely, and therefore, not taking the risk is very important.

Growth Investing

This means going for stocks in well-established companies; companies are already doing well and attracting many potentials. This means that everyone is already running for these investments, and they are doing pretty well. There is even evidence of how well the companies are doing. People investing in this have a lot of faith in this investment because they expect that it only keeps growing. People buying in this type of investment do not mind buying at a high price because they know that they will sell even more significantly than they bought it. Therefore, what happens here is that you go for big and well-known companies. These are companies that are well known and have been in the market for a long time.

The right investment strategy, however, still goes back to an individual. What works for an investor is very important instead of relying on what worked for others. It may have worked for others, but not work for you. However, it is good to involve all the strategies as you make decisions as an individual investor.

CHAPTER 3:

Debit And Credit Spreads

Debit Spread

A debit spread entails buying a high premium choice while offering a low premium choice in the same category and the same protection, which leads to debit from the trader's account.

Alternatively, a debit spread (usually utilized by beginners to option techniques) requires purchasing an option with a more significant premium and selling an alternative with a reduced premium. The place that the premium settled for the lengthy choice of the spread is much more than the premium gotten from the written choice.

A debit spread leads to a high quality debited, or maybe given, out of the trader's or perhaps investor's account whenever the position is opened compared with a credit spread. Debit spreads are used mainly to offset the expenses related to owning long feature positions.

For instance, a trader buys, one could place a choice with a strike price of $20 for $5, and also instantly sells one could put an option with a strike price of $10 for $1. Thus, he paid $4 and $400 for the swap. In case the trade is from the money, the max loss of his is lowered to $400 instead of $500.

Types of Debit Spreads

- Bear put spread requires two transactions and a bearish strategy, which are buying one at the money put option, and the selling of 1 on the money put option. This is done because the trader is betting that the associated asset's price movement will go down. Profit is earned when the associated asset's price is the same as the put option's strike price.

- Bull call spread, a bullish strategy that includes two transactions: buying one at the money call option, and selling 1 out of the money call option. A trader implements this strategy when they think that the associated asset's price movement will go up modestly. Profit is gained when the associated asset's price is the same as the short call option's strike price.

- Butterfly spread, a neutral strategy that involves three transactions whereby the trader buys 1 in the money call option, sells two at the money call option, and buys one on the money call option. Profit is gained when the price of the associated asset remained the same on the date of expiration.

- The reverse iron butterfly is a volatile strategy that involves four transactions. These transactions are selling 1 out of money put option, buying one at the money put option, buying one at the money call option, and selling 1 out of money call option. Profit is gained when the price of the associated asset falls.

Credit Spread

Spreads can be classified in different ways. Credit spreads are distributed strategies that involve total receipts of premiums, while debit spreads include total payments of premiums. It entails promoting a high premium choice while buying a low premium choice in the same category or the same security, which leads to a credit on the trader's account.

The premium got from the written choice is higher than the premium settled for the long option, leading to a high quality credited into the trader or maybe the investor's account whenever the position is opened. When traders or investors utilize a credit spread program, the maximum revenue will be the total premium. The credit spread leads to an income once the options' spreads narrow.

For instance, a trader tools a credit spread program by composing the 1st March call option with a strike price of $30 for $3 plus concurrently purchasing the 1st March call option with $40 for $1. Since the typical multiplier on an equity choice is a hundred, the web premium received is $200 because of the swap. Moreover, the trader is going to profit when the spread tactic narrows. A bearish trader expects stock prices to reduce, therefore, and buys call choices (long call) in a particular hit cost and offers (short call) the same amount of call options inside the same category, and the same expiration in a reduced hit selling price. In comparison, bullish traders expect stock prices to increase, and consequently, purchase call options in a particular hit cost and promote the same call options.

Types of Credit Spreads

- Bear call spread, which is a beginner-friendly strategy. It employs a bearish outlook that relies on the price of the associated asset decreasing modestly. Profit is gained by finding the difference between the option premium and the commissions paid. Loss occurs when the asset price increases below the strike price.

- Bull put spread is a beginner-friendly strategy with a bearish outlook that substantially decreases the associated asset price. Loss occurs when the asset price drops below the strike price.

- Iron butterfly spread, which involves four transactions. The options trader is buying 1 out of the money call option, selling one at the money call option, buying 1 out of the money put option, and selling one at the money put option, all with the same expiration date and associated asset. This is a complex strategy that is not recommended for beginners.

- A short butter spread entails three transactions. The transactions are buying 1 out of the money call/put option, selling 1 out of the money call/put option, and buying one at the money call/put option with the same expiration date and associated asset. This is also a complex strategy that is not recommended for beginners.

CHAPTER 4:

Options Strategies: Going Long vs. Going Short

As an options trader, you will often hear the terms going long or having a long position and going short or taking a short position. The positions are opposites. Both terms refer to what the investor owns, and what they need to own to be effective at options trading.

Having a short position means that the investor does not own the assets being associated with the option. For example, there may be an option for 100 shares, but the investor doing the selling does not own the shares.

Long Position

On the other hand, having a long position means that the investor owns the option's asset. For example, an investor who bought and added 100 shares to their portfolio has a long position. This investor likely bought this asset, which can be stock, commodity, or currency, expecting that the value will rise. This is known as having a bullish view. A bullish view describes an investor's characteristic of pursuing an asset with the feeling that it will appreciate because they wish to limit any potential losses.

There is another view that can affect if an options trader decides to hold a long position. The trader may try to make a profit, but the fall of an asset's value. This can be advantageous because the trader can obtain an option to sell that asset at a price that is advantageous to them.

The long position refers to whether or not the trader will hold a long call or long put option as it relates to options trading. This is dependent on the associated asset attached to that contract. Having a long call option means that the trader expects that the asset's price will go up so that he or she can benefit in that regard. The option allows the trader to buy that asset at the strike price to fulfill the upward trend.

With a long-put option, the trader expects the asset to depreciate so that he or she can purchase the right to sell that asset at a predetermined price.

In both cases, the long position does not in any way refer to the period. The focus is entirely on the associated asset and who owns it. The person who owns the asset is called the long position holder.

One of the biggest benefits of a long position is an option of this nature locks in the strike prices. Losses are limited because the trader can base his or her bets on historical market performance.

Unfortunately, there are disadvantages to going long. Firstly, the financial market may become volatile and cause abrupt price changes. This may not be for the benefit of the options trader. Secondly, the option may reach its expiration date before the advantage the options trader hopes to achieve is realized.

Simple Going Long Strategies

Of course, there are very complicated, going long strategies that can be employed, but it is best to start and get a lay of the land as a beginner.

Long Call

This strategy is considered by options traders who want to make a profit from an asset that increases in the price above the strike price. This is often considered so that the trader does not have to buy the asset outright to potentially profit without having to take on the significant risk of owning that asset.

This option can also afford the trader access to assets he or she cannot afford to purchase at that time. This is a common practice in accessing stock. Having the option to purchase is less expensive than purchasing the stock outright.

Here is a summary of how a long call works:

Outlook: Bullish.

Risk: The premium paid.

Potential profit: Unlimited. It increases as the price of the asset increases.

Break-even price: The sum of the strike price and premium paid (strike price + premium paid).

An example of a successful long call is as follows:

An option trader buys 100 shares of stock that he believes will increase in value within the next few months. Each share costs $20. He believes the shares will go up by at least $10. Therefore, he buys the option at a strike price of $20 plus a cost of $2 for each stock, which totals $22 per stock.

As long as the stock goes above $22, this long call option is profitable to the trader. For every dollar the stock goes higher, the trader will profit $100. As the stock price increases, so do the option value. Therefore, the trader can sell the option to lock in his profit.

The best thing about such an option is that the asset can infinitely increase in value, leading to massive profits. This is why long calls are a popular way to bet on rising stock prices.

In this case, this is also a risk that the trader will lose their investment in the cost of the premium and associated fees. The asset may not become advantageous before the expiration date arrives, and thus, the option becomes worthless to the trader.

Long Put

This type of option gives the trader the right to sell the associated asset at the strike price on or before the expiration date. The options trader makes a profit from the asset, decreasing to a price below the strike price. As you can see, this is very similar to the long call, and only differs in that the trader is betting on the fact that the asset's value will fall below the strike price on or before the expiration date.

Long puts are a great way of protecting the value of assets that you already own.

Here is a summary of how a long put works:

Outlook: Bearish (Falling prices).

Risk: The premium paid.

Potential profit: Unlimited. It increases as the price of the asset decreases.

Break-even price: The difference between the strike price and premium paid (strike price - premium paid).

An example of a successful long put is as follows:

A company is trading stock at $50 per share. An options trader feels that the price of this will fall to at least $30 per share within the coming months, and so seeks a put option with a strike price of $50 that had an expiration date of 2 months. He buys 100 shares and pays $150 to purchase each $50 share. The option is priced at $5 per share, and so the trader pays $500.

The trader was right, and the stock's price depreciated to $25 per share before the expiration date. With the current stock price, the trader with the put option will be in the money because the stock's intrinsic value has risen. Let's say that this value is now $1500. The trader can sell the stock for that price. The trader will make a profit of $1000 after removing his investment of $500.

This scenario's great advantage is similar to the advantage in the long call, hence why this too is a popular way of betting on declining stock values. As a result, a long put is a great option if the trader expects the asset's price to fall significantly before the expiration date arrives. If the price falls only a little or not, the trader may be in the money only slightly, which is not profitable, or worse, it may not even return the premium the trader spent.

Short Position

The second position in Options Trading is the short positions. It is the opposite of the long position explained. The investor anticipates a decrease in the price of the option to gain profit. Executing a short position is not as easy as when you buy an asset.

Using a short stock position as an example, the investor expects profit if the stock drops price. This is possible by borrowing some shares from a particular company's stakeholders while selling it at the current price.

With this, the investor has an open position for the number of shares they bought with the broken. Remember, this stock has a particular timeframe before it will be closed.

By chance, the stock price drops, the investor has the right to buy the number of stock shares lower than the total price he sold them.

The excess cash for this trade is the profit of the investor.

Most investors find it hard to understand the idea behind short selling; however, it shouldn't be complicated. To clarify this, the example below can make things clear for you.

Assuming the stock of NCE is currently sold for $50 per share. For some reason, you anticipate a fall in the stock price and decide to sell short of making a gain from your anticipation. How then should your short sale look like?

- You place a margin deposit as collateral to your broker to give you a loan of 100 stock shares.

- With the loaned shares given to you, you sell them at the price of $50 per share. With this, the share isn't yours anymore; however, in your account, you have $5,000 ($50 x 100 = $5000). In this situation, you are short of stock because you are in debt of 100 shares to your broker.

- Assuming your expectation that the price would fall happens gradually. After some weeks, the price dropped to $30 per share. Furthermore, you expect the price not to go any lower, so you decide it's time to close the sale.

- You then bought the 100 shares at the price of $30, amounting to $3,000. You decide to repay the 100 shares of stock you borrowed from your broker.

- With the 100 stocks, you could make a profit of $2,000 by activating a short trade. When your broker loaned you the shares, you received $5,000 ($50 x 100 =$5000), and after buying, you were able to pay back your loan amounting to $3,000. Amount received ($5,000) – Amount Paid ($3,000) = Profit ($2,000).

Short positions are usually given to accredited investors because it requires a high level of trust between the broker and the investor to execute this deal. It doesn't matter if the short is executed; the investor must place collateral that the broker will use in exchange for the loan you want to take.

Short Call

A short call position is activated when an investor sells a call option. The position is the opposite of the long call. The seller is in a better position to profit short call position is activated, and the value of the asset or stock drops.

Alternatively, when the investor triggers a put option, the seller profits if the option traded is higher than the predetermined option price.

Options trading comes with varieties of long and short positions for you to adopt during trading. A knowledgeable investor who understands all individual positions' advantages and disadvantages will always be ahead of the market.

However, if you are a new trader, don't rush to apply for these positions. Understand each position before making an effort to combine it into your trading strategy.

CHAPTER 5:

The Flexibility Of Options

Flexible trade options, or FLEX options, are non-standard choices that permit both the essayist and buyer to arrange different terms. Terms that are debatable incorporate the activity style, strike value, lapse date, just as different highlights and advantages. These alternatives also offer financial specialists the chance to exchange for a more significant scope with extended or disposed position limits.

- FLEX alternatives are a particular sort of choice contribution outrageous debatable adaptability.

- FLEX represents an adaptable trade choice.

- These alternatives don't have standard statement streams yet distribute cites just according to popular demand.

Understanding Flexible Exchange Option (FLEX)

FLEX alternatives were made in 1993 by the Chicago Board Options Exchange (CBOE). The other options focus on the counter (OTC) market of file choices and give clients greater adaptability. It currently exchanges on different trades just as the CBOE.

Besides permitting both the purchaser and vendor to tweak contract terms precisely as they would prefer, FLEX alternatives give different advantages. These advantages incorporate security from counterparty hazards related to over-the-counter exchange. The Options Clearing Corporation ensures exchanges (OCC), as are other trade exchanged choices.

The market is additionally increasingly severe and straightforward for expanded liquidity. An optional market permits purchasers and dealers to counterbalance positions before termination. This optional market evacuates a portion of the dangers of exchanging off-trade markets.

A huge contrast between FLEX alternatives and conventional choices is that FLEX options don't have a consistent statement stream. Subsequently, the age of a statement for FLEX options happens just when a solicitation for a quote (RFQ) is made.

In 2007, The CBOE propelled CFLEX, an Internet-based, electronic exchanging framework for file and value FLEX options. Merchants enter day by day arranges into the FLEX electronic book.

Parts of a FLEX Option Contract

The base size for a FLEX alternative is one agreement. Strike costs might be in penny increases, and may likewise be in what could be compared to a level of the hidden stock.

The portrayal of premiums might be in the estimation of explicit dollar sums and are ordinarily in penny increases or basic stock rates.

A termination date can be any business day and can be future-dated similar to 15 years from the exchange date. Lapse styles might be American or European. American lapse takes into consideration practice whenever before the agreement closes. European lapse grants practice just at the termination date.

Value FLEX choices, the two puts, and calls settle with the conveyance of stock portions whenever worked out. Record FLEX choices will settle in real money.

Position Limits for Flexible Exchange Options

There are no position limits for FLEX alternatives on important market files, including the Dow Jones Industrial Average, Nasdaq-100, Russell 2000, S&P 500, and S&P 100. Be that as it may, there are revealing prerequisites if position sizes surpass sure edges.

As far as possible for expansive based Index FLEX Options, other than those recorded above, are 200,000 agreements, with contracts being on a similar side of the market for each given list.

There are no position limits for value or ETF FLEX alternatives, even though there are announcing prerequisites.

CHAPTER 6:

Strangles Strategies

The strangle strategy will help you benefit from the trade no matter the direction of price movement. Here too, you will buy put and call options of an equal amount, and both of them should have the same expiration date. The only difference between strangle and straddle is that in the straddle strategy, both the options' strike prices were the same, whereas, in the case of strangle, the strike prices are different. The trader believes that there will be movement in a specific direction, or there is a greater chance for the stock to move in that direction. Still, even then, the trader wants to protect his position if there is a negative move. The two types of strangle strategies are the long strangle, and the other is the short strangle.

Profit
or Loss

LONG STRANGLE

35   45

$0

30   40   50

Stock Price
at Expiration

-$200

Profit
or Loss

SHORT STRANGLE

$200

Stock Price
at Expiration

$0

30   35   40   45   50

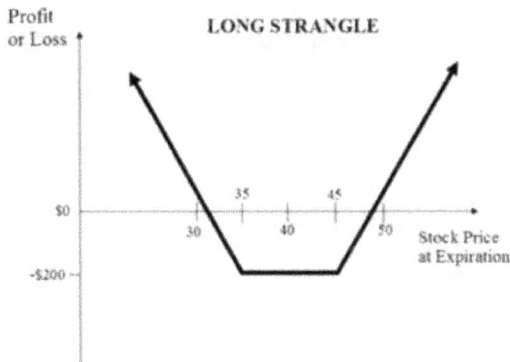

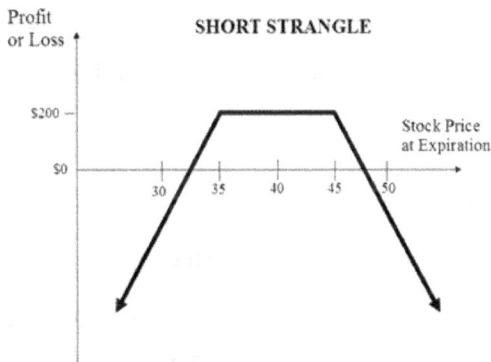

The long strangles main aim is to help you make a profit whenever the stock undergoes a huge change in price in either direction.

This strategy comprises one long put that has a lower strike price, and a long call with a greater strike price. The expiration dates of these options' underlying assets are the same, whereas the strike prices are different. This type of strategy is based on net debit, and it will be profitable if the price of the underlying stock decreases, and goes below the lower breakeven point or goes above the upper breakeven point.

On the upside, the potential for making profits with this strategy is unlimited, and on the downside, it is substantial. On the other hand, the potential loss in this type of strategy is capped by the strangles total cost and any commissions that you had to pay.

You will incur a loss with this strategy if you trade fewer volatile stocks because for the stock price to move beyond the put or the call, there has to be high volatility. Only seasoned veterans and higher-ups should approach using this strategy because it might seem relatively simple to you initially, but executing it in the right way is not everyone's cup of tea. Your forecasting ability should be sharp and advanced for you to profit from this strategy.

Traders usually implement this strategy when they think that there will be an abnormally huge move in the stock price because of a significant event or news. For example, if an earnings announcement is approaching, then you can consider running this strategy before that. But unless you are dead sure about that huge swing in price, I think you should stick to long straddle instead of long strangle. I know that it is costlier to run a straddle, but the breakeven points are closer than that of the strangle, and so the stock can outrun those points even when the move is not that huge.

What Are the Advantages of This Strategy?

Look at some of the advantages that this strategy has to provide you:

- The first advantage of the long strangle is that it is less expensive than the long straddle. Now, this strategy deals with out-of-the-money options, which you already know have a lower premium than the options that are at-the-money.

- The second advantage is that the maximum loss that a trader can incur with this strategy is limited. This maximum loss situation happens when at the time of expiration; the price of the underlying stock is trading in a range between the strike price of the call option, and the put option you just bought. In such a scenario, the options will reach their expiration, and they will expire worthlessly. The initial debit that you had to pay to enter the trade will be lost.

- The potential for profit in this strategy is unlimited, which is one of the most significant advantages. This happens when there is a huge move in the price of the underlying stock to crosses and goes beyond the strike price of either option.

One disadvantage associated with this strategy, and that is, to make a profit from this strategy, the movement has to be quite huge. Consider also the time decay because, with time, both the options lose their value, and the factor of time decay is double because of the involvement of both call and put options.

This strategy is quite similar to that with just one difference because a slight adjustment has been made to make this strategy cost-effective. To ensure that you bring home profits from this strategy, the increase in the call options' value has to be more than the decrease in the value of the put options. You can also make a profit when the increase in the value of the put options is more than the decrease in the value of the call options. The strike prices you choose for this strategy can be of any desired combination, but it is usually established near an at-the-money option towards the mid-point of the strike price.

You should also ensure that the stock has low implied volatility so that the price of the options is low, but there should be a probability for the stock to make an explosive move in a direction. Suppose you consider from your intuitive point of view. In that case, you will realize that implanting the strangle strategy is a very lucrative option because you will make a profit irrespective of the stock's direction of movement. But both of your selling and buying decisions have to be perfectly timed to benefit from this strategy truly.

In simpler terms, volatility expansion is one of the main things on which the strangle strategy's success depends. The sharp price movement can be brought about by anything like earnings reports, important announcements, or even a lawsuit's verdict. In some cases, the traders prefer to benefit from a low volatility situation and purchase the strangle at that time so that when after the announcement, the volatility increases, they can sell the option and make a huge profit.

But you have to decide whether you have to implement a long straddle or a long strangle, and the decision will have to be made after judging the probability of the stock to make a huge movement and the amount of the cost you want to bear.

The maximum risk is the net debit invested at the beginning of the strategy. The maximum reward is unlimited because the underlying stock can show downward or upward movement without any limits. To calculate the upside breakeven, add the net premium paid with the strike price. For the downside breakeven, subtract the net premium paid from the strike price.

CHAPTER 7:

Straddle Strategies

This is a strategy you could use to profit if the stock rose high, and you also earned profit if the stock crashed. The strategy used to accomplish this is called straddles. These strategies are great for use in volatile markets.

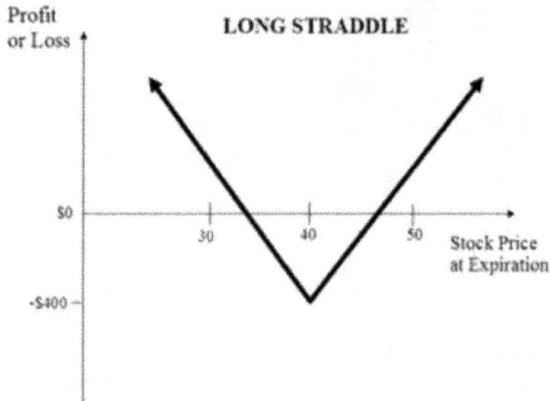

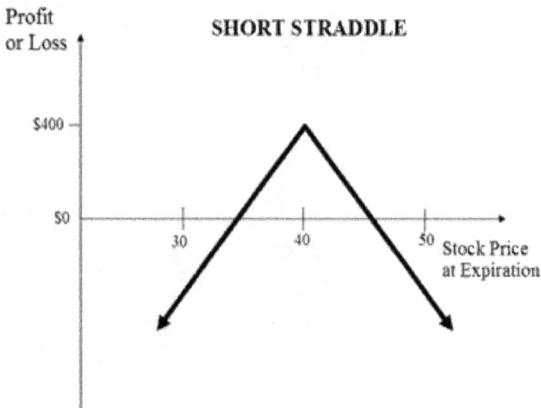

This is also a two-legged strategy designed to take advantage of price breakouts of stock, without regard to the breakout's direction. Like a strangle, a straddle will also involve buying a call option and a put option on the same stock, and with the same expiration date, simultaneously.

However, a straddle differs from a strangle in one key aspect. To set up a straddle, you will also set up the trade so that the call option and the put have the same expiration date. The chart for a straddle is shown below. This narrows down the range over which there are losses. Maximum loss on the trade would occur if the stock price were equal to the strike price at option expiration.

The same type of strategies should be employed when using straddles rather than strangles. This means you want to enter your position over a week's time frame up to maybe three or four weeks before a big event like an earnings call. Over the period between your purchase and the earnings call, the straddle will gain value from stock movements, regardless of whether the stock's price moves up or moves down.

If the stock price increases, the straddle's value will increase because of the call option that is a part of the trade. However, it could also lose value due to the put option that is a part of the trade. The price has to move one way or the other so that the share price is higher than the strike price + cost of the position or lower than the strike price minus the position's cost. Remember that for a straddle, the call option and the put option have the same strike prices.

For our example, we are entering the trade 21 days before expiration. The call is $6.93, and the put is $7.89, so the total cost to enter the position would be $14.92. Let's say that there is an earnings call when the option is five days to expiration.

Now, by 15 days to expiration, in anticipation of the upcoming earnings call, the share price might have moved a bit. Let's suppose that the market expects a good earnings call, so share prices are going up. If the share price went up to $237, this is a modest gain that, despite time decay, will help the value of the call option. It has risen from $6.93 to $7.36. However, the put option has lost some value due to time decay combined with the modestly higher stock price, and it's now going for $5.33.

Our plan, however, is to hold the position until the earnings call. Remember that earnings call also impact volatility. We are setting the implied volatility at 33% for this exercise, but as we get closer to the earnings call, that value will rise.

Now ten days to expiration, which would be five days to the earnings call in our scenario. The share price has risen to $240 share since the markets are expecting good news. Implied volatility has also increased to 37%. The call has jumped to $8.37, but the put is now down to $3.63.

There are only two days left until the earnings call, moving forward to just seven days to expiration. Now implied volatility has risen to 45%. The share price has increased steadily with the passing days and now stands at $245. Under these conditions, the call is $12.26, and the put is $2.25. The total value now is $14.51, and it cost $14.92 to enter the position, so we have a mild loss at this point, but it should be ignored. We need to hold the position until the earnings call.

Later that day, the stock is at $247, and the implied volatility has risen to 50%. The call is now $14.32, and the put is $2.30, so our position is now worth $16.62. Since it cost $14.92 to enter the position, we are now at a point of profitability to the tune of $16.62 - $14.92 = $1.70. If you wanted to, you could sell it now for a profit of $170. You'd find an eager buyer without a doubt because most traders would be anxious to get in on the trade before the actual earnings call.

Finally, we reach the earnings call. It beats expectations by a surprising margin, and the price of the stock jumps $23 a share in after-hours trading. At market open, the call option is worth $36.01, and the put is worth pennies on the dollar. At this point, the put option is worthless, but the call option has gone up so much in value that we are looking at a profit of $36.01 - $14.92 = $21.09 per share, putting us in a position where we can sell for a total profit of $2,109.

If the stock continued climbing the morning after the earnings call, which sometimes happens, we could earn even more profits. If it went to $280 a share by the afternoon, the call option would be worth $45. In that case, we'd have another $900 in total profits on the trade. Of course, you are taking some risk. The longer you hold the position. The stock might start declining a bit or stop rising. And if you hold it overnight, you are going to get hit with time decay. The put option is entirely worthless at this point, but it doesn't matter.

Suppose that instead, the price had plummeted. Our hypothetical company might have missed expectations by a large margin, and rather than rising by a huge amount, it could drop to $210 a share instead. The beauty of the straddle is that in this scenario, we make a profit as well. This time, the call option would be completely worthless on the trading day after the earnings call, but the put option would be worth $24.99, giving us about a $1,000 profit. The more the stock drops, the more profit we would earn. The same holds for a strangle, but remember that the call and put options have different strike prices, and there might be a wider range over which the stock needs to move to earn profits.

CHAPTER 8:

Covered Call

It is a trading strategy for beginners, which is an excellent way to get started selling options. By covered, we mean that you've got an asset that you own that covers the potential sale of the underlying stocks. In other words, you already own the shares of stocks.

The basis of this strategy is that you don't expect the stock price to move very much during the options contract's lifetime, but you want to generate money over the short term in the form of premiums that you can collect. This can help you develop a short-term income stream; you must structure your calls carefully.

Setting up covered calls is relatively low risk, and will help you get familiar with many options trading aspects. While it's probably not going to make you rich overnight, it's an excellent way to learn the trade tools.

Benefits of Covered Call Options

- A covered call is a relatively low-risk option. The worst-case scenario is that you'll be out of your shares but earn a small profit, a smaller profit than you could have made if you had not created the call contract and sold your shares. However, you also get the premium.

- It allows you to create income from your portfolio in the form of premiums.

- If you don't expect any price moves on the stock in the near term, and plan to hold it long term, it's a reasonable strategy to generate income without taking much risk.

Risks of Covered Call Options

- Covered calls can be a risk if you're bullish on the stock, and your expectations are realized, and there is a price spike. In that case, you've traded the small amount of income of the premium with a voluntary cap of the strike price for the possible upside you could have had if you had held the stock and sold it at the high price.

- If the stock price falls, even though you still get the premium, it will be worthless unless they rebound over the long term. You shouldn't use a call option on stocks that you expect to be on the path to a significant drop in the coming months.

In that case, rather than writing a covered call, you should sell the stocks and take your losses. Alternatively, you can keep the stocks to see if they recover over the long term.

Covered Calls Involve A Long Position

To create a covered call, you need to own at least 100 shares in one underlying equity. When you make a call, you will be offering potential buyers a chance to buy these shares from you. Of course, the strategy is that you're only going to sell high, but your real goal is to get the premium income stream.

The premium is a one-time non-refundable fee. If a buyer purchases your call option and pays you the premium, that money is yours. No matter what happens after that, you've got that cash to keep. If the stock doesn't reach the strike price, the contract will expire, and you can create a new call option on the same underlying shares. Of course, if the stock price does pass the strike price, the contract buyer will probably exercise their right to buy the shares. You will still earn money on the trade, but the risk is you're giving up the potential to earn as much money that could have been earned on the trade.

If the stock price doesn't exceed the strike price over the contract's length, you get to keep the premium, and you get to keep the shares no matter what.

In reality, in most situations, a covered call will be a win-win situation for you.

Covered Calls Are A Neutral Strategy

It is also known as a neutral strategy. Investors make covered calls for stocks in their portfolio, where they only assume small moves over the contract's lifetime. Moreover, investors will use covered calls on stocks that they expect to hold for the long term. It's a way to earn money on the stocks during a period in which the investor expects that the stock won't change much at a price and have no earning possible from selling.

How to Create a Covered Call Option

To create a covered call, you'll need to own 100 shares of stock. While you don't want to risk a stock that is likely to take off shortly, you don't want to pick a total dud. There is always someone willing to buy something, at the right price. But you want to go with a decent stock so that you can earn a decent premium.

You start by getting online at your brokerage and looking up the stock online. When you look up stocks online, you'll look at their "option chain," which will give you information from a table on premiums available for calls on this stock. You can see these listed under the bid price. The bid price is provided on a per-share basis, but a call contract has 100 shares. You have an option with the premium you want to charge.

You can set any price you want. Of course, that requires a buyer willing to pay that price for you to make money.

A more reasonable strategy is to look at prices people are currently requesting for call options on this stock. You can do this by checking the asking price for the call options on the stock. You can also see prices that buyers are currently offering by looking at the bid prices.

To sell a covered call, you select "sell to open."

An Example Of A Covered Call

Let's say that you own 100 shares of Acme Communications. It's currently trading at $40 a share. Over the next several months, nobody expects the stock to move very much, but you feel Acme Communications has solid long-term growth potential as an investor. You sell a call option on Acme Communications with a strike price of $43 to make a little bit of money. Suppose that the premium is $0.78 and that the call option lasts three months.

For 100 shares, you'll receive a total premium payment of $0.78 x 100 = $78. You pocket the $78 no matter what happens.

Now let's say that the stock drops a bit in price over the next three months so that it never comes close to the strike price, and at the end of the three months, it's trading at $39 a share.

The options contract will expire, and it's worthless. The buyer of the options contract ends up empty-handed. You have a win-win situation. You've earned the extra $78 per 100 shares, and you still own your shares at the end of the contract.

Now let's say that the stock does increase a bit in value. Over time, it jumps up to $42, and then to $42.75, but then drops down to $41.80 by the time the options contract expires. In this scenario, you're finding yourself in a much better position. In this case, the strike price of $43 was never reached, so the buyer of the call option is again left out in the cold. On the other hand, you keep the premium of $78, and you still get to keep stock shares. This time since the shares have increased in value, you're a lot better off than you were before, so it's a win-win situation for YOU, even though it's a losing situation for the poor soul who purchased your call.

There is another possibility that the stock price exceeds the strike price before the contract expires. In that case, you're required to sell the stock. You still end up in a position that isn't all that bad, however. You didn't lose any actual money, but you lost a potential profit. You still get the premium of $78, plus the earnings from the 100 shares' sale at the strike price of $43.

A covered call is almost a zero-risk situation because you never actually lose money even though you missed out on an opportunity if the stock price soars. You can minimize that risk by choosing stocks you use for a covered call option carefully.

For example, if you have shares in a pharmaceutical company rumored to be announcing a cure for cancer in two months, you probably don't want to use those shares for a covered call. A company with more long-term prospects but probably isn't going anywhere in the following months is a better bet.

CHAPTER 9:

Strategies for Selling Covered Call

Bear Put Spread Strategy

The bear put trade seeks to take advantage of bearish markets. In contrast to bullish markets with varying degrees, bearish markets tend to have far lesser degrees of strength. While a bullish market can be classified on many levels ranging from slightly bullish to extremely bullish, bear markets would lend themselves to only two or three such classifications.

The reason for this is straightforward. The general public and the large majority of institutional activity is focused on the long side of the market. Therefore, when these institutions conduct their buying campaigns, you will see a greater degree of fluctuation within a stock as it goes up. The very fact that a larger number of traders are involved produces more price behavior scenarios, resulting in a more significant number of trend strength levels.

In contrast, bear markets have far lesser traders involved, and they tend to quickly get to the point. You won't find a bear market trying to make up its mind as it leans towards moving downwards. Distribution movements that often occur before a bear trend don't last very long and bear trends run faster and exhaust themselves sooner than bull trends.

The point of this is to say that you need to be on your toes with bear markets. The bear aims to do the same thing, but there are slight differences in the way they play themselves out.

Execution

The bear put his two legs to it:

- Long put at or near the money.

- Short put out of the money below the long.

The primary profit here is the long put, which will appreciate as the stock price decreases. The short put aims to reduce the cost of carrying the long put via the premium earned upon writing it.

AMZN is currently trading at 1833.51, and let's assume that the bear trend in this stock is beginning to show signs of slowing down, and it is approaching a strong support level that it is unlikely to go past. You'll learn the signs of identifying all these things later. For now, commit them to memory, and make a note to refer to them later.

The closest at the money put in the 1835 strike price near month put, which asks $53.80 per share. This is a large portion of our trade. Now, we need to determine which level is appropriate for the short. Well, we've seen from our chart that a strong support level is close by that is unlikely to be breached. Why not use this as a low level?

Let's say this is $1800. The bid for this put is $39.85 per share. Here's how the math works out:

Cost of entry = Cost of long put - Premium earned from short = 53.8-39.85 = $13.95 per share.

Maximum gain = Difference between long and short put strike prices = 1835-1800 = $35 per share.

The maximum loss is the same as the cost of entry since the changes in the premiums of both puts will offset one another. As the price rises, the long put will decrease in price while the short will decrease by the same rate, thus giving us a profit that offsets the loss on the long leg of the trade.

By this point, hopefully, you're familiar with working out the math of spread trades and can see how the dynamics of it work. In terms of adjustment, it works the same way with the bear put as it does with the bear call. If the price rises and takes your long put out of the money, you need to determine whether your analysis was correct.

If you think it holds, you can close out the short, which will give you a profit to offset the large portion, which will also be closed out. Establish a new spread or keep the short at the same level. Note that you can close out your long put, and go long again at a higher price without touching the short if you wish to keep it at the same level.

The criteria you need to follow for adjustment are the same as with call spread trades. Your decision will be based on the technical analysis factors you see, and how well you can deduce conclusions from them. There is another choice you face, now that you've learned how the bear put works, and that is whether you should choose a bear call spread or a bear put spread.

Both strategies seek to take advantage of similar market conditions, so which one should you choose? Before we get into the evaluation of this, we need to look at bull put spreads first.

Bull Put Spread Strategy

Bull put spreads are useful to take advantage of sluggish uptrends or sideways movements with an upward tilt to them. In doing this, they're pretty similar to bull call spreads, and the mechanics of this trade is pretty straightforward, as you'll see.

Execution

Two legs make up the entirety of this trade:

- Short in the money or at the money put

- Long out of the money put a few levels below the short

The short put is the leg that takes advantage of the rise in prices. The long put covers your downside in case market sentiment doesn't work out in your favor. Once you enter the trade, you'll earn the put premium, and will have to pay to enter the long put.

The difference between the two is your cost of entry, as well as your maximum gain.

Your maximum loss is the difference between the strike prices of both legs. If the stock price falls and brings your long put into the money, your downside is capped at that level. Therefore, when you enter this trade, you will receive money or a net credit. Contrast this with the bear put, which is a net debit. In other words, you pay money to be in the trade.

Let's look at an example to flesh this out further using AMZN. The market price is the same, but this time, our environment is different. It is a bullish environment that is sluggishly moving upwards. Our closest at the money put to short is the 1835 level, which puts $53.30 per share in our pocket.

Let's assume the support level below is at 1800, so the cost of going long here is $40.40. Thus, our cost of entry is:

Cost of entry = Cost of long put - Premium from short put = 40.4-53.3 = -12.90 per share (we receive this much as credit). This is the maximum gain as well.

Max loss = Short put strike price - long put strike price of = 35$ per share.

As you can see here, just like the bear call, the reward to risk ratio is skewed, but the reasons for entering this trade despite this are the same as in the former case. In case you wish to adjust your trade, your criteria are the same as before; that is, it depends on your faith in your technical analysis.

Put Calendar Spread Strategy

In direct contrast to the call calendar spread trade, the put calendar spread trade seeks to take advantage of a decline in a stock's price. This is less widely used than the call calendar spread. Either way, it works in the same manner by creating a horizontal spread between the same strike prices but different expiration dates.

If you anticipate AMZN to decline to 1800 after a month, you can buy the put of the near or far month, which will cost you $40.40 per share. Since you reason that AMZN is not going to hit this mark within this month, you can buy the front-month put at the same level, which will net you $21.95 per share.

This creates a net debit of $18.45 per share and is your maximum loss. Your maximum gain is subject to the same conditions as with the call calendar spread. That is to say, it is unlimited, and depends on whether the price hits your shorter-term put before it expires. Either way, this horizontal spread is a great way to take advantage of bearish market movements.

Choices

While the horizontal spreads offer us pretty easy choices between the two of them, with the call spread for bull markets and the bear spread for bear markets, things get a bit murkier with the vertical spreads. Two sets of strategies exist to take advantage of similar market conditions, so which one is better?

Usually, such a question is often answered by looking at which one makes more money. The reality of the situation is a bit different, however. The money you make on the trades can be affected by the strike price levels, and you can manipulate a net debit spread trade to yield more than a credit spread by just fiddling with the strike prices, and hoping for some luck. No, a more sophisticated set of rules is needed.

Thankfully, risk management principles give us the way out. Volatility is the most significant risk that plagues option traders. It isn't volatility itself but changes in volatility. You'll often find options traders abandon vertical spreads before major announcements because option prices go haywire thanks to current fluctuations in the markets. This is, in fact, true for directional traders as well, but they at least have the choice of betting in a particular direction and profiting from a huge move.

Ideally, options traders seek to enter at times of low volatility, and exit during high times. This is because the volatility factor in the option price produces significant increases in premiums. It is this precise number that gives us hints as to which strategy to choose.

Purpose

Despite looking to take advantage of similar market conditions, the net credit and debt strategies' underlying principles are very different. A net debit strategy seeks to reduce the premium a trader pays to enter the trade. As premiums shoot up during periods of high volatility, a net credit strategy will end up with the trader footing hefty bills for inflated option premiums.

Sure, they will be able to make a greater profit on a credit spread. However, if volatility results in them paying a huge amount in the first place, the decrease in volatility will reduce the extent to which the premium will move. This is where debit spreads are so useful. They take the volatility out of the equation, with one leg canceling the other.

CHAPTER 10:

Iron Condor

The Iron Condor (IC) is a strategy that requires you to have some prior knowledge of the Greeks, and how you can go about taking advantage of them.

This is why before trading this; it helps to simulate this strategy extensively and to never go live with it unless you know everything to do with it inside out.

The most important education you will receive in this strategy will be when you deal with live prices.

The trade itself has four legs to it:

- An out of the money (OTM) short put

- An OTM long put with a lower strike price

- An OTM short call

- An OTM long call with a higher strike price

The income-generating portions of this trade are legs 1 and 3.

These will earn you a premium, and subtracting the premium paid from the premium received will define your maximum profit. In terms of structuring the trade, it works like this.

Around your market price that is on top of it, and to the bottom you'll write an OTM call and an OTM put. Above the call and put, you will buy an even further OTM call and put.

Thus, you short the lower OTM strikes and buy even more OTM strikes.

Iron Condors

SHORT IRON CONDOR

SETUP:
OTM LONG PUT
OTM SHORT PUT*
OTM SHORT CALL
OTM LONG CALL*

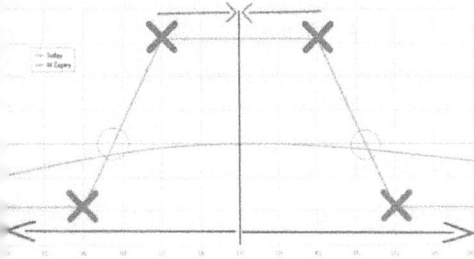

LONG IRON CONDOR

SETUP:
OTM SHORT PUT
OTM LONG PUT*
OTM LONG CALL
OTM SHORT CALL*

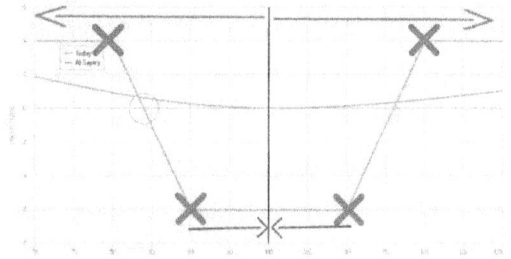

Execution

Before jumping in and placing your orders, you need first to identify possible candidates. More than anything else, this is what will define your trade's success. The idea is to set up an IC when volatility is low. In other words, you're sure that the price is going to be within a tight channel, and isn't going to break out in a particular direction.

Hence, when searching for stocks, you need to look for those in a ranging environment. The ideal stocks are entering a tight range, preferably in the middle or towards the end of a trend. Stay away from ranges that occur at the end of trends because they produce many upswings and downswings, and increase the implied volatility.

The implied volatility is a good measure for you to use. Do not rely on this directly since it is merely a measure of what other traders think will happen to volatility. So, if you enter based on a low implied vol but see that the price is headed into a trend, stick with what the chart says. Let the other traders have their implied volatility numbers and suffer with them.

When speaking of implied volatility, it is about comparative values. So, you need to look at the current values to the historical ones and determine whether they're on the higher or lower side.

Next comes the timing of the trade. How long should you target to keep this open? Unlike the last strategies, you should seek to open an IC at least fifty to sixty days out from expiration. You want to give yourself this much time because as the option moves closer to the expiry date, its gamma is going to increase. Gamma increasing implies a volatility increase, which will reflect itself in how the option is priced.

When you trade close to expiry options with this strategy, the option prices will reflect a fast-moving gamma and volatility. Thus, it will take just a small change in prices for the option premiums to go against you. You're liable to find yourself in a position where the underlying price has decreased, but your short call has increased or stayed at the same premium.

This makes it difficult for you to adjust the trade. Any subsequent small increase in the underlying will put you in the red, and the subsequent movement from the short put will not compensate for the value lost.

A good method to adopt is to look at all the Greeks to see how they're printing relative to their historical values. All four are related to one another, so if there is a truly low volatility situation, you're in for a great chance at a profit.

This is why traders love the IC. It is complicated enough to put off any newbies who couldn't be bothered to spend the time learning it. It is just easy enough to present the intermediate to advanced trader with good and high probability opportunities.

The IC is called a net credit trade, meaning you receive money when you enter the trade. This also happens to be your maximum gain, while your maximum loss is far more significant. Estimating your maximum loss is the key to figuring out how much of a position you need to take. This is where it gets a bit tricky since option pricing requires you to take volatility into account. How can you predict what volatility is going to be in the future to predict a price?

You'll see what I mean when we look at an example using numbers. For now, understand that you need to establish the long legs of the trade before the short legs. If you set the short call and put it before the other two, you're likely to trigger all sorts of warnings from your broker, and they might even suspend your account for some time since it looks like you have no idea what you're doing.

So, take it slow and easy. Most important of all is determining that the volatility conditions are good for entering and executing the IC.

Example

Let's stick with GOOG for this, assuming it is in a range and that all the indications are for it to enter a low volatility period for the following month or so, or the near future at the very least. The current market price is 1229.

For our long legs, let's say we buy the November 15th, 1245 call. This will cost us 41.40. Next, we set up the long-put leg for November 15th. Let's choose a strike price of 1215. This costs us 38.50 to purchase.

Now, it's time to set up the short legs of the trade. Remember, each leg's strike prices need to be closer to the market price than the long ones. For the put, we choose 1220 as the strike and earn 38.6, and for the call, we choose the 1240 call. This yields us 39.20.

So, our cost of entry is:

Cost of entry = sum of premiums received - the sum of premiums paid = 2.10 per share.

Now to figure out our maximum loss. The trade works in our favor as long as the price remains between the two short legs' strike prices. If it exceeds the strike price of either one of the long legs, that is, if it moves either long into the money, we're faced with our worst-case scenario.

To figure this out is to estimate the intrinsic value in such a situation. So, if GOOG were to rise past 1245, the long option will gain at least a dollar in intrinsic value per unit rise.

Furthermore, the short call will now be in the money, and its premium will have decreased by at least $5 (since that's the spread between the two legs).

Our short put and long put will still be out of the money, but both will have lost their values by at least the difference between their strike prices and the current worst-case market price. In this case, they will decrease by at least $29 in total. This is your minimum worst-case scenario level. Keep in mind that this is just an estimate.

There are volatility factors that will affect the price of the options. Therefore, it is a good idea to apply a safety factor of some sort to this value and then use that to determine your position size. How much of a factor should you apply? This is difficult to say because every stock has its volatility history. So, you ought to play around with it on simulation before going live.

Now that we've set up the trade, we need to think about the exit. Our goal is not to let these expire or hold them until the two-month period is up. After all, it will be tough to find a stock that remains in a range for that long. Besides, the volatility will go all over the place if it stays in a range for that long. No, we aim to capture the decay of time value.

The usual exit point is when the options have thirty days remaining on their expiration dates. Since you're starting, targeting far month options (sixty days or more left till expiry) is your best bet.

When you become more comfortable executing these trades, you can take weekly options that expire a month plus a week away. Thus, your trade will be active for a week.

Easy Formula

Many traders will target half of the maximum profit level to fix an exit point. For example, if your trade was projected to earn you a maximum of 10%, traders will make a profit when it hits the 5% mark. This method has its advantages and disadvantages.

The biggest advantage is that it makes it very easy to monitor your trade. Using an online option calculator or even the one in your trading terminal, you can input the prices and calculate your current profit. When your net gain moves to half of what you received as credit, you take the trades off the table and exit the position entirely.

The biggest disadvantage is that beginners are prone to take this far too early. Remember, you need to stay in the position to capture the greatest time value decay. If your position moves into a loss early, you need to adjust it, and this is a whole other ball game.

A lot of traders are intimidated by adjustment, and this is why they'll exit quickly. From a reward to risk standpoint, taking half of your intended profits over and over will reduce your winnings because you'll be leaving too much on the table. However, take enough trades, and this even out. So, it's a tradeoff at the end of the day.

CHAPTER 11:

Options Pricing

Options traders need to comprehend extra factors that influence an option's price, and the complexity of picking the right technique. When a stockbroker becomes acceptable at foreseeing the future price movement, the person may believe it is a simple change from options, but this isn't accurate. Options traders must deal with 3 shifting parameters that influence the price: the underlying time, volatility, and security. Changes in any of these factors affect the option's value.

Option pricing hypothesis utilizes factors (exercise price, stock price, interest rate, time to expiration, volatility) to value an option hypothetically. It estimates an option's reasonable value, which traders join into their techniques to maximize profits. Some ordinarily utilized models to value options are Black-Scholes, Monte-Carlo, and Binomial Option Pricing. These speculations have wide margins for error because of deriving their values from different assets, typically the cost of an organization's basic stock. There are scientific formulas intended to compute the fair, reasonable value of an option. The broker inputs known factors and finds a solution that depicts what the option should be worth.

The essential objective of any option pricing model is to compute the probability that an option will be worked out or be in-the-money (ITM) at lapse. Basic asset value (stock value), interest rate, exercise price, time to expiration, and volatility, which is the number of days between the computation date and the option's exercise date, are usually utilized variables that are input into logical models to derive an option's hypothetical fair value.

Here are the general impacts that factors have on an option's cost:

Strike Price and Underlying Price

The value of puts and cuts are influenced by changes in the fundamental stock cost in a generally clear manner. When the stock cost goes up, calls should gain value since you can purchase the underlying asset at a lower cost than where the market is, and puts should diminish. In like manner, put options should increase in value, and calls should drop as the stock value falls, as the put holder gives the right to sell stock at costs over the falling market cost.

That pre-determined price to purchase or sell is known as the option's exercise price or strike price. Suppose the strike price permits you to purchase or sell the basic at a level that allows for a quick profits purchase, discarding that exchange in the open market. In that case, the option is in-the-money (for instance, a call to purchase shares at $10 when the market cost is currently $15, you can make a prompt $5 profit).

Like most other monetary resources, options costs are affected by prevailing interest rates and are affected by interest rate changes. Put option and call option premiums are affected contrarily as interest rates change lose value while calls benefit from rising rates. The inverse is genuine when interest rates fall.

The impact of volatility on an option's price is the most difficult concept for beginners to comprehend. It depends on a measure called statistical (also known as historical) volatility, SV for short, looking at past value developments of the stock over a given timeframe.

Option pricing models necessitate the trader to go in future volatility throughout the life of the option. Normally, options traders don't generally know what it will be, and need to guess by working the pricing model "in reverse". The merchant knows the cost at which the option is trading and can inspect different factors, including dividends, interest rates, and time left with a bit of research. Subsequently, the main missing number will be future volatility, which can be evaluated from different information sources.

Factors That Affect An Option's Price

You cannot price an option until you realize what makes up its worth. An options trade can turn into a mind-boggling machine of legs, numerous orders, Greeks, and adjustments. However, if you don't have the foggiest idea about the essentials, what are you attempting to achieve?

When you take a look at an option chain, have you considered how they generated every one of those prices for the options? However, these options are not created randomly, but rather calculated out utilizing a model, for example, the Black-Scholes Model. We will dive further into the Black-Scholes Model's seven components, and how and why they are utilized to determine an option's cost/price. Like all models, the Black-Scholes Model has a shortcoming and is a long way from perfect.

History Of The Black-Scholes Model

The Black-Scholes Model was distributed in 1973 as The Pricing of Options and Corporate Liabilities in the Journal of Political Economy. It was created by Myron Scholes and Fisher Black as an approach to evaluate the price of an option after some time. Robert Merton later distributed a subsequent paper, further extending the comprehension of the model. As with any model, a few assumptions must be comprehended.

- The rate of profit for the riskless asset is constant.

- The more the option will be worth, the underlying follows, which expresses that move in an unpredictable and random path.

- There is no riskless profit, arbitrage, opportunity.

- It is possible to lend and borrow any amount of money at a riskless rate.

- It is possible to purchase or short any amount of stock.

- There are no charges or costs.

The model has seven factors: strike price, stock price, interest rates, types of option, dividends, time of expiration, and future volatility.

Stock Price

If a call option permits you to purchase a stock at a pre-determined cost later on, then the higher that cost goes, the more the option will be worth.

Which option would have a higher worth:

- A call option permits you to purchase TOP (The Option Prophet) for $100 while it is trading at $80 or

- A call option will enable you to buy TOP for $100 while it is trading at $120

Nobody will pay $100 for something they can purchase on the open market for $80, so our option in Choice 1 will have a low worth.

All the more alluring is Choice 2, an option to purchase TOP for $100 when its worth is $120. In this circumstance, our option worth will be higher.

Strike Price

The strike price follows the same lines as the stock price. At the point when we group strikes, we do it as in-the-money, at-the-money, or out-of-the-money. When a call option is in-the-money, it implies the stock price/cost is higher than the strike cost. The stock price is not exactly the strike price when a call is out-of-the-money.

A TOP call has a strike of fifty while TOP is presently trading at $60. This option is in-the-money.

The stock price is not exactly the strike price when a put option is in the money. A put option is out-of-the-money when the stock price is greater than the strike price.

A TOP put has a strike of twenty while TOP is presently trading at $40. This option is out-of-the-money.

In-the-money options have a greater value contrasted with out-of-the-money options.

Type Of Option

This is likely the easiest factor to comprehend. An option is either a call or a put, and the option's estimation will change appropriately.

- A call option gives the holder the option or right to purchase the basic at a predefined cost within a particular timeframe.

- A put option gives the holder the option or right to sell the hidden at a predefined price within a particular timeframe.

If you are long a call or short a put, your option value increments as the market moves higher. Suppose you are short a call or long a put your option value increments as the market goes lower.

Time To expiration

Options have a constrained life expectancy; thus, their worth is influenced by the progression of time. As the time to expiration upturns, the value of the option increments. As the time to termination draws nearer, the value of the option starts to diminish. The value starts to quickly diminish within the last 30 days of an option's life. The additional time an option has till termination/expiration, the option needs to move around.

Interest Rates

The interest rate has a nominal effect on an option's value. When interest rates rise, a call option's value will rise, and a put option's value will decrease.

To drive this idea home, how about we take a look at the dynamic procedure of investing in TOP while trading at $50.

- We can purchase 100 shares of the stock altogether, which would cost us $5,000.

- Instead of purchasing the stock altogether, we can get long an at-the-money call for $5.00. Our all-out expense here would be $500. Our underlying cost of money would be littler, and this would leave us $4,500 leftover. Also, we will have a similar prize potential for half the risk. Presently we can take that additional money and invest it somewhere else, for example, Treasury Bills. This would create a guaranteed return on our investment in TOP.

The higher the interest rate, the more appealing the subsequent option becomes. In this manner, when interest rates go up, calls are a superior investment, so their cost likewise increments.

On the other side of that coin, if we look at a long put versus a long call, we can see an impediment. We have two options when we want to play an underlying drawback.

- You can short a hundred shares of the stock that would produce money into the business, and earn interest in that money.

- You long a put which will cost you less money by and large, but not put additional money into your business that produces interest income.

The higher the interest rate, the more appealing the primary option becomes. Accordingly, when interest rates rise, the value of put options decreases.

Dividends

Options don't get dividends, so their value varies when profits are discharged. When an organization discharges dividends, they have an ex-dividend date. If you own the stock on that date, you will be granted the dividend. Additionally, on this date, the estimation of the stock will diminish by the number of dividends. As dividends increment, a put option's value likewise increments, and a calls' value declines.

Volatility

Volatility is the main evaluated factor in this model. The volatility that is utilized is forward. Forward volatility is the proportion of implied volatility over a period later on.

Implied volatility shows the "simplified" development in a stock's future volatility. It discloses to you how traders think the stock will move. Implied volatility is constantly communicated as a percentage, non-directional, and on a yearly premise.

CHAPTER 12:

Dividends

With dividend stocks, you only invest once and earn forever! Passive income refers to the type of income that you create even when sleeping it is something desired by many. This income generation method can build your wealth either by helping cover your monthly expenses or reinvesting. Dividends are the best fit as a passive income source. This is because the income is sustainable, requires little maintenance, grows faster than inflation, and can also be tax-advantaged. It might take you time to get a reasonable amount of dividend income, but time is always on your side in this case.

What Are Dividends?

Dividends, just like many other financial subjects, are simple on the surface but very complicated underneath. From a surface point of view, dividends are paid to give out a company's earnings to its shareholders. You must be aware that being a shareholder in a company that pays dividends `entitles you a share of its profits. A perfect dividend policy is beneficial to both the company and the shareholder. Many investors chose to invest in great dividend-paying companies as the basis of their portfolio.

This technique is referred to as dividend growth investing. In this case, growth refers to the growth of dividend payments over some time. Since the 1990s, the average annual dividend increase is always around 6%. This, however, is not a fixed rate; it isn't unheard of for companies to have a yearly dividend of 10% or more!

Dividend Investing

If you are not sure about dividend investing is, this topic is for you. As mentioned earlier, dividends refer to the way companies share success with their shareholders. It is like a portion of the total earnings paid out you as the shareholder. You can choose to get your dividends in the form of cash or more shares. You might want to know what dividend dates are? For instance, a company can declare a dividend of Y dollars. The day this information was relayed is known as the declaration date, the time is, however not that important.

When looking at a dividend, there are two significant dates you should know. Ex-Dividend Date: you must own a stock before this date so that you can receive the bonus. Payment Date: This is the day money is paid to shareholders. The Record Date is technically the date you need to be recorded as a shareholder to be entitled to dividends. This date is always two business days after the ex-dividend date: this is solely because trades take two days to settle. It has lesser importance to an investor than the ex-dividend date. It is, however, good to know what the record date is. Additionally, pay more attention to the ex-dividend date!

Comparing Stocks for Dividend Investing

There are two ways you can look at dividends and determine how good they are. Both of them are pure math. The dividend yield is a certain percentage showing the amount of money the profit is compared to the share price. The higher the amount, the better: this means you earn more passive income out of your investment. For example, if the average dividend amount of the company is 3.46%, it means you earned $3.45 in dividends for every $100 you invested.

The second you can use to determine whether the dividend ID proper is the dividend payout ratio: this refers to the paid dividends and divided by the company's total earnings. You should ask yourself if the company makes sufficient profit to cover for the dividends, they promised you. Look at the dividend growth rate. Most companies tend to increase their dividends over time, and this metric establishes the rate at which they do so.

When to Reinvest or Not to Reinvest

Remember, when we deliberated the two options when it comes to when acquiring your dividend? You should consider that in this situation. It can be easier two chose to base on that because you will know what your investment objectives are.

Considering your age, this could be the best decision as you will take advantage of the compounding magic.

Dividend Growth Investing: Case Study

In this case, we make up a situation to show you just how great dividend growth investing can be. Let us assume you bought $10,000 worth of Toyota shares on the New York Stock Exchange in early 1999. Below is how much you will have at the moment. 243 share of Toyota worth $41.02 each $4296.34 in passive income in the following 12 months ($1.22 per share annually) 2.96% dividend yield ($296.45/$10,000).

You should note that the example had to be set in the USA Stock Exchange because all these financial calculators online-only support American tickers. Fast forward to 2019; you made five times your initial investment mainly due to capital gains. Interestingly, your passive income grew even more, multiplying itself more than seven times the initial amount. The outcome (passive income growth) was due to two factors: dividend reinvestments and dividend pay raise.

How to Start Chasing Dividend Income

Below are the three steps you can take to start chasing your dividend income.

Pick a Type of Account

The first thing you need to do is pick a type of account you prefer to work with. Dividends are taxable in some countries, meaning you could benefit from keeping them legally registered accounts like RRSP or TFSA. Deciding where to place your investments can be a very confusing thing. Below is what you need to take away from this subtopic. TFSA: applies Canadian, American, and other international stocks, and ETFs RRSP: Refers to Canadian, American, and other foreign stocks, and ETFs.

Unregistered Accounts: Canadian, American, and other international stocks, and any margin trading engagements (paying maximum taxes on dividends, and handle riskier investments to get capital investments just in case an investment goes wrong). Generally, the fee charged on profits is lower than that charged on a regular income. There are, however, many rules and exceptions, especially regarding US Stocks.

Choose a Stockbroker

As you might know, the broker needs to provide the type of account you required in Step 1. You will also want a broker that offers a DRIP when chasing dividends. You should, therefore, be careful with the kind of broker you are opting for. Preferably, go for brokers that support registered accounts like RRSPs and TFSAs.

Decide between ETFs and Stocks

The essential dividend growth investing pertains to picking individual stocks using the metrics we deliberated earlier. There are plenty of ETFs in different countries that mainly focus on dividend income, and have little management expenses. While ETFs charge a fee that digs into the returns, it is a shallow maintenance strategy. You don't need to look at individual companies and their payout ratios. Instead, what you need to focus on is the distribution you earn and the yield it provides you.

Keep on Contributing and Investing

This is a continuous process that does not stop once you purchase your first stocks. The case study we used above focused only on a one-time investment tracked over 20 years far along. You should, therefore, be making regular deposits, and slowly be picking up even more ETFs, and dividend stocks. This will result in your passive income stream growing even at a faster rate. Ideally, you can use a DRIP where possible for most of your investment life to accelerate growth.

CHAPTER 13:

Technical Analysis For Options Trading

Traders often use a set of tools known as technical analysis to help them make better trades. Specifically, it can help you detect developing trend reversals in stock charts. This information can help you get into, and out of your trades at the best possible time. Technical analysis involves a wide range of tools.

Studying Trends with Moving Averages

The most important thing on a stock chart that a trader will look for on a stock chart is a trend reversal. If you are looking to profit from call options, then what you will look for is a relatively low stock price or a stock price in decline, and then wait for it to show signs of a reversal. This is going to help you buy low and sell high. Once you have entered a position, the technique is to study the charts looking for the coming reversal once the price has peaked, so you can exit your position.

Moving averages are the easiest tools to use for this purpose. It takes several periods of stock data, and at each point, it calculates the average out to a fixed number of points. The definition of a "point" is up to the individual trader, and it could be an hour, four hours, a day, or a week. It could even be five-minute intervals. If you plan on trading an option over 30 days, you will probably be looking at using days for your time frame. In that case, a 9-period moving average would calculate the average of the closing price at each day, using the past nine days to do the calculation.

To spot trend reversals, traders rely on moving averages with different periods (but they will use the same definition of the period, be it a day, week, or five minutes). You could use a 9-period moving average, and a 20-period moving average. Alternatively, you might use a 50-period moving average, and a 200-period moving average.

A longer-period moving average will give you more information on the historical pricing level of the stock in question. Different types of moving averages are going to treat this in different ways. A simple moving average will do a standard mathematical average of all data points. So, if we had a 9-period simple moving average for closing prices of Apple, on a particular day, it might calculate:

SMA = (212.41 + 213.11 + 212.50 +214.29 + 215.72 +216.01 + 217.22 + 217.50 + 216.95)/9.

Many traders are completely content to use the simple moving average, but if you look at how it's calculated, you should note that all prices are treated the same. This is objectionable because if you are looking to make a trade, recent prices will be more important than history, older prices. We certainly want information from the stock's historical pricing level, but it is more recent prices that are going to have the most impact on our trading decisions. Many traders use weighted moving averages that give more weight to recent closing prices, and less weight to closing prices in the past. Two very popular weighted moving averages are used, the Hull moving average, and the more popular exponential moving average.

To detect a trend reversal, you will use two moving averages on your stock chart of the same type, but with different period lengths. You can use nine days exponential moving average with 20 days exponential moving average.

The first rule is known as a golden cross. This happens when the short-period moving average curve crosses above the long-period moving average curve. This tells you that the stock is likely to be entering an upward trend. In the example below, a 50-day simple moving average, and a 200-day simple moving average are used. Notice that after the golden cross (the 50-day moving average crossing above the 200-day moving average); the stock enters a relatively long-term upward trend.

This tool's beauty is that it is very simple to use, it is also something that a beginning trader can understand quite easily.

Of course, stocks are not always going up. Otherwise, everyone would be rich. So, we have to know how to spot the development of a downward trend in prices. A so-called death cross indicates this. In a death cross, the short-period moving average curve crosses below the long-period moving average curve.

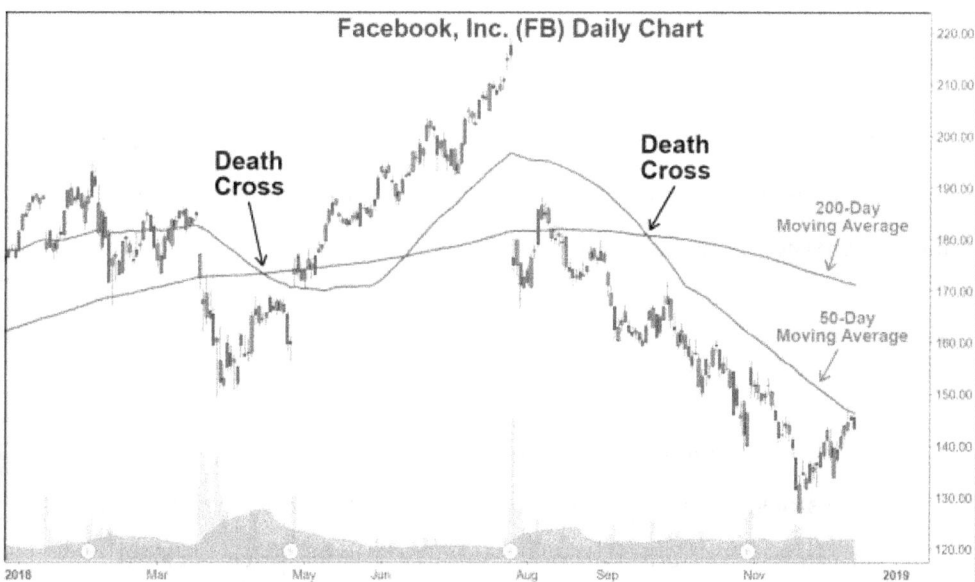

The question now is how to use crosses of moving average curves with options trading. When you are looking to get into a trade, you should add the appropriate moving averages to your charts, and then use a golden cross or a death cross as a signal to enter or exit trades.

For call options, you want to enter a trade when there is a golden cross. Then, when the chart shows a death cross, exit your positions. It's that simple.

For put options, you will do the opposite. That is, you will wait to enter your trade until you see a death cross. For options traders, since you can profit, either way, a "death" cross is also a signal for profits, but with using put options. Then you hold your position until you've either reached a level of profit you are comfortable with or you see a golden cross, indicating a coming trend reversal.

Remember that with options, the expiration date and time decay are always lurking in the background, so you don't necessarily want to wait for another crossing to occur before exiting your positions.

Momentum

One of the most essential concepts that stock traders look for is momentum. Price momentum occurs when many traders are either buying or selling a stock, pushing prices strongly in one direction or another. The tool you can use to study the momentum of a stock price is called the Relative Strength Indicator. You can add this to your stock charts to help you study the best times to get into and out of positions to maximize possible profits.

The relative strength indicator will be displayed below your stock chart. It is a curve that can go between 0 to 100. Typically, the values 0-30 and 70-100 are what traders are looking for on the chart. When the curve goes into the range of 0-30, this means that a stock is "oversold." That is, traders have sold off too many shares, pushing prices down to a level that makes it likely that new traders will find the stock now an attractive buy, so they are likely to start loading up on the stock and pushing prices upward again. The lower the RSI gets, the stronger this signal is.

When the RSI goes into the range of 70 and above, this indicates overbought conditions. In this case, frantic purchasing of the shares has pushed prices up too high, and traders are likely to start getting out of the stock because they want to get out before the price drops when there is a large selloff.

The RSI should not be taken in isolation. A good way to use it is to use it in conjunction with the moving averages. So, if you see oversold conditions with the RSI, together with a golden cross, that indicates that stock prices are likely to start moving upwards.

If the RSI shows overbought conditions, and you also see a death cross, this can be taken to indicate that stock prices are likely to be pushed in a downward direction soon.

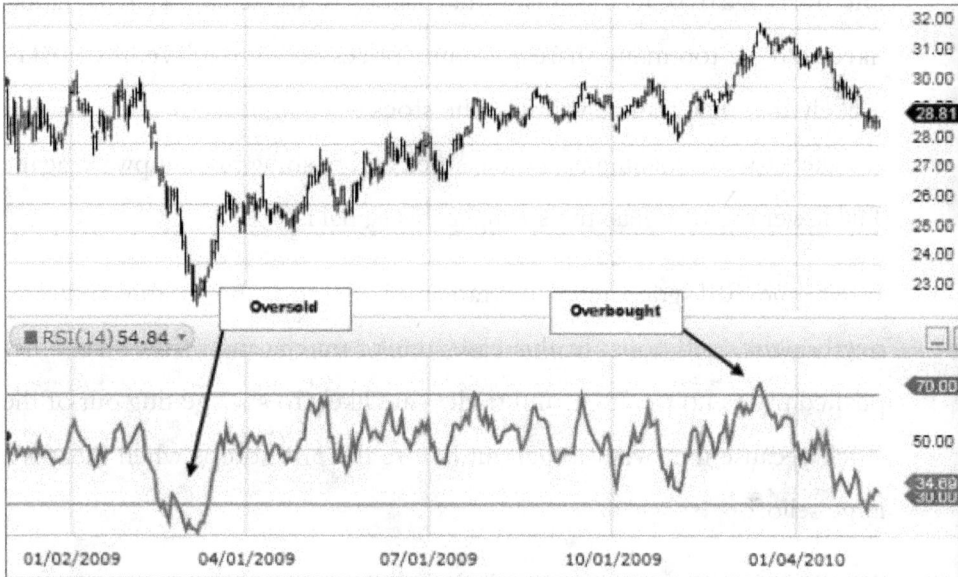

Support and Resistance

The concepts of support and resistance are important for options traders to understand, especially if you are interested in trading iron condors. These concepts are not complicated, so most readers will have no problem grasping them.

In many cases, a stock is not going to be shooting up or crashing to the floor. In fact, over most periods of the stock market, stocks will be bouncing around in the same price range, and possibly gradually increasing or maybe decreasing, but over relatively short periods staying the same.

When this happens, we say that the stock is "ranging." The values that the stock prices range between are called support and resistance.

Support is the low-price level. So, while the stock is ranging, it will dip down to the support price level but not go below it. After it drops to support, it will probably start rising again. You want to look for a price that the stock reaches at least twice over the time frame you are looking to declare a support price.

Resistance is the upper price level that the stock cannot break above. Again, you want to look for the stock price to move up to the resistance price at least twice over the time frame. So, while the stock is ranging, it will drop down to support, then bounce around, go up to resistance, drop back down to support again, and keep repeating this process. Stocks can do this for extended periods.

For options traders, when the price drops to resistance, this is a time for those trading call options to enter their positions. Put option traders would sell their positions at this point. When the price goes up to a resistance level, then traders investing in call options should sell their positions, while this is a point that you would be looking to enter a position if you were interested in trading put options. The rules are pretty simple.

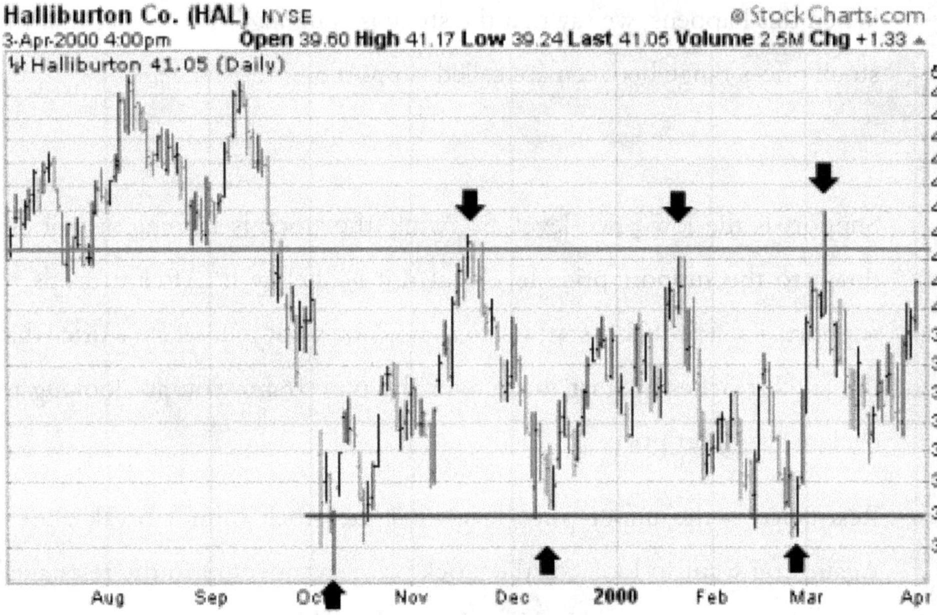
Halliburton Co. (HAL) NYSE
© StockCharts.com
3-Apr-2000 4:00pm
Open 39.60 High 41.17 Low 39.24 Last 41.05 Volume 2.5M Chg +1.33
Halliburton 41.05 (Daily)
Aug
Sep
Oct
Nov
Dec
2000
Feb
Mar
Apr

Breakouts

Breakouts occur when a stock suddenly gains momentum in one direction or the other, so the stock price will break out above resistance or drop below support. In this case, you are likely to be looking at forming a new, long-term trend that can help you make profits either with call options or with put options. If there is a breakout above resistance, you want to invest in call options, and ride the upward trend for as long as possible.

To take advantage of breakouts, an options trader should be paying close attention to the financial and economic news. In particular, keep an eye on any news about specific companies that you are interested in investing in.

Trendlines

A simple method of analysis that you can use to "trade with the trend," whether it is up or down, draws trendlines on your charts. A trendline will help you determine where the stock price is going to end up in the future. You cannot take this to be an absolute fact, and it is only a guide for what might happen. To draw a trendline for an upward moving stock price, start at a local low price, and then draw the line upwards, touching the local dips in the curve up. At least 2-3 minima should touch your line. The end of the line (which we are assuming extends past the current price) will give you an estimate of where the price will be at a future date. To draw a trendline for a downward trending price, use the same procedure, but use the local peaks in the price to determine your line.

VeriSign, Inc. (VRSN) Nasdaq Nat. Mkt.
-Mar-2000 4:00pm Open 251.00 High 251.00 Low 244.50 Last 248.50 Volume 1.7M Chg +2.81
VeriSign 248.50 (Daily)

Conclusion

The options trading crash course is all about options trading. I hope this guide will teach you everything you need to know about options trading, from basics, why people trade options, and how you trade options. It will teach you everything you need to know on this important topic so that you can start making money right now with options trading without having any knowledge at all. You will find out precisely what kinds of investments there are available, and exactly how much your broker will charge for each one so that you can choose the one that is best for your situation.

With options, you can make money by selling an asset at a specific price and buying it back after rising in price. It's an exciting and profitable way to gain financial freedom. The options market is the largest and most liquid market globally, which means that it is also very popular. Options trading is an attractive option for anyone looking to make money from their investments. It's a way of investing in stocks or other securities without actually having to buy them.

Options trading is a great way to make money while watching the markets. Although options trading can be a complicated process, there are plenty of resources to help you get started.

This can be a great way to make money, but it's essential to do your research and know what you're doing. It is one of the most fun and lucrative forms of investing, but it's also one of the most challenging.

The goal of options trading is to buy stock or other assets at a price you think will go up in the future.

Options trading has become a popular investment strategy for many. Both beginners and experienced traders can benefit from the basics of options trading. The essential part of options trading is understanding the different options available and how to use them.

www.ingramcontent.com/pod-product-compliance
Lightning Source LLC
Chambersburg PA
CBHW071717210326
41597CB00017B/2518